Smiling with Teeth

poems by

Harley Anastasia Chapman

Finishing Line Press
Georgetown, Kentucky

Smiling with Teeth

Copyright © 2020 by Harley Anastasia Chapman
ISBN 978-1-64662-264-1 First Edition
All rights reserved under International and Pan-American Copyright Conventions. No part of this book may be reproduced in any manner whatsoever without written permission from the publisher, except in the case of brief quotations embodied in critical articles and reviews.

ACKNOWLEDGMENTS

A special thank you to the publications that have previously featured these poems, in one form or another:

"The Truth" *Contemporary Verse 2*
"Hawkmother" and "Life Study" *2River*
"In This Story" *Soundings East*
"Bloodletting" *Bridge Eight Press*
"Featherlungs" and "the answer to that question" *Columbia Poetry Review*

As well as much love to those who helped me develop these poems through workshop &/or support: Lisa Fishman, David Trinidad, Morgan Peacock, Ricki Cummings, Laura Waltje, Leslie Eidson, Nick Weaver, Leonard Morrison, Nicole Covington, & Eddie Weber. I deeply appreciate each of you.

Publisher: Leah Maines
Editor: Christen Kincaid
Cover Art: Harley Anastasia Chapman
Author Photo: Nicole Covington
Cover Design: Elizabeth Maines McCleavy

Printed in the USA on acid-free paper.
Order online: www.finishinglinepress.com
also available on amazon.com

Author inquiries and mail orders:
Finishing Line Press
P. O. Box 1626
Georgetown, Kentucky 40324
U. S. A.

Table of Contents

The Truth 1

In This Story 2

Love Poem to My Mother 3

Hawkmother 5

A Coat for Nesting Dolls 6

Life Study 7

In This Story pt. 2 8

A Case for Bones 9

304 E 1st St. 10

Astro-Inheritance 11

Bloodletting 12

The Shape of a Hand 13

Featherlungs 14

the answer to that question 15

The Bad Orange 16

To The Point 17

In This Story pt. 3 18

To-do 19

Portrait of an Ill Man 20

The Same Man 21

A Christmas Story 22

An Order of Protection 23

From Here 24

To my mother: an apology, a hug, a prayer
To my grandmother: my entire heart
To my sister: three red candles & an open door

The Truth

He tucked me under your bed
as a mandrake, fed me sugar plums
from his mouth while you fevered.
The day he tried to de-root me
I screamed & screamed
& have kept on screaming.

In This Story

The witches live together in their witchness,
that is to say an aversion to men,
whether chosen or simply how it all worked out.
There is too much red meat in their diets
because the head witch,
that is to say the matriarch, the beginning,
had a lack of it in her childhood
& is making up for lost meals.
They say *I love you* too much
for the same reason.
In this story there is never a second husband
or heavy-eyed boyfriend who pounds on the door
at 4:00 am. The witches still adopt a little boy
(but it really isn't an adoption, is it?
He is one of them) & imbue him
with all the virtues of the witch—
Do not forget where you come from. Do not
put a man before your mother, sister, child.
Do not let them into our house.

Love Poem to My Mother

I know you as the patron
saint of broken
things, a collection piled
high as grandma's basement
knick-knacks. When
I was eight you told me
to write letters to TLC
asking for an Xtreme Makeover
for my mom & you'd laugh
after but you asked
every time. You'd say
I was lucky
I got my dad's
genes, always eating
always skinny. You'd say
you were happy
I wouldn't have to be
fat like you. You cried
every Christmas
you could only afford
socks, took your car title
& traded it for too little
even though I told you
not to. You said
get a good education
& get a good job
so I can make money
because you don't want
me to ever worry
about money. You want
me to be happy & I can't
be happy if I can't support
myself. When I was 15
we were driving
& it was winter & you
were stressed about bills.

You said you should
crash the car, spare us both
the life of being left
& being poor. You're
ashamed you said
those things, but I know
sometimes you still think
those things. Like Everclear
I'm trying to buy
you a new life. One day
I'll buy you a new life.

Hawkmother

I'm trying to turn my mother into a hawk.
Her coffee is too loud,
she prefers wings made of rabbit.
I tell her all the redemptions of the hawk,
how he wings gold at sunset
how he spots prey for x miles.
She tells me I should brush my hair.
At night I break the bird
& put its body limp under her pillow.
By morning she is pink clay.
When her boyfriend comes home water-eyed
she is on him, a king's bird.
I watch her clean her teeth
as if she has a bone to pick with.

A Coat for Nesting Dolls

Carry my mother's sadness,
a quilted overcoat bloated with rain.
Patch holes with the thread in our knees,
threads caught on the devotion, Scala Sancta
pine needles that wedge deeper every stair.

Pass the coat from mother to daughter
to daughter like uterine lining.
Feed it intention & goose feathers.

Sometimes we all wear it at once.
I climb inside my sister, inside my mother,
inside grandma with her feet in her mother's urn.
We leave our bodies hanging on the kitchen wall.

Stitched in the collar a rusty A.
Shame placed where you wouldn't see
unless we chose to show
or let it slip. I am the slippiest, always
wear the coat inside out.

Tell the person I love I'm sorry
for the coat, for how unflattering it is.
In it I'm a badger, a stout ugly angry thing.
I pull the hood down low & all he sees is teeth
hanging yellow as my face.

December is the hardest. Crawling
in someone else's sadness, which is also your own.
A co-op of coat that never dries or freezes, stays
wet as a mop, stiff as the headstone
standing watch in the garden.

We don't waste time or spells trying
to lighten what must remain heavy.
Thicken our nails, shape them dagger
& fuchsia. Eat cereal with cream,
lick every fat-rich drop.

Life Study

I have made my life a study
of silence, the culmination of your
warnings. I hang lilac from the bramble
in our backyard, mother,
drench the peonies in insecticide.
When their heads hang
carpenter bodies fall like snow.
That's what they get, mother.
Don't they know what is ours?
A family of groundhogs have
burrowed near, I saw them
waddling in a line by the garage.
A mother & three kits.
Do you remember that house
you lived in for a summer,
how the owner caged
the groundhog before he could
undermine the front porch?
How the creature clawed against
the wire & it was so hot that day,
his paws blood-shiny, mouth
frothing. We tried to shade
him, provide water
but we couldn't become things
he could trust. I wanted so badly
to free him but couldn't bring myself
to open the cage door.

In This Story   pt.2

The head witch lights her husband on fire
before he gambles away her home.
He dies not in a succession of deaths, but a blaze.
Spared the vegetation of one stroke
followed by another, he squats in the Ouija board
& planchets for supper.
Miller Lite vigils are held every
Wednesday, Thursday, Friday night.
In this story nobody leaves the house for good
& death is just a settled debt.
The bills are paid before the groceries bought
or the groceries aren't bought at all.
Eyes are collected in mismatched Tupperware
& lined up on the fridge.

A Case for Bones
> *after Maggie Smith*

I've been thinking on good bones
& what makes up the bones
& what makes the bones good.
I know my bones are good
because they came from my mother
& my grandmother before her.
The skeleton I've inherited
invites heavy winds & doesn't bow.
We weren't made to keep out.
There are wide spaces between
our ribs where you can settle
for a night or a year.
There are no doors here.
Nothing to keep you in.
We built around empty space
& know it well. It's a comfort
to feel it creaking. To know
it is a part of our construction.
We don't fear bad weather
or the loss of things
that keep us warm.
My grandmother taught me
to open all the windows
when a tornado threatens.
Invite it in for tea, ask it to leave
the important bits unbroken.
If it wants to demolish you,
let it try.

304 E 1st St.

This is what makes the land our own:
the gnomes rooting up the backyard.
In the front, a pit of snakes.
We all flock back like a v falling into itself,
our retreat when new ground fails.
A kitchen sink you have to stoop over,
an L of a living room.
That big window, thick enough
to keep everything out.
You can't abandon the home front
when there are ghosts who need tending.
It is ours in every way that matters.
On paper it's a draw.
If anything keeps my grandmother
inching past one more Christmas
it's the stubborn draw of land to blood.
The bank will try to take it all away.
"Not while I'm alive," she says.
"Not while I'm still kicking."

Astro-Inheritance

I am tracing my skin,
looking for my mother.
The constellations
blooming brown & bleach
are Sagittarius.
She was never my sun
or moon or rising,
but here she is
drawing an arrow
over the blade of my
right shoulder.
Here she is
stamping her hoof
in my spine.
I spent twenty years
blanketing my back
to keep her sleeping.
I didn't want
to hold my mother
as stardust & prophecy.
To watch her lines
blur & grow.
The doctor says be wary
of melanoma.
He refuses to see
the mapping of a matriarch
or mother presence,
just a born
predisposition.

Bloodletting

On black nights we drive southwest
an hour-fifty on I-80, find the pockets
of wild pocked enough to see the stars.

This is the land that milked us safe
passage in its breast—the womb of sky above
holds my grandmother. She is Libra

scaling out the hours & she is barn owl
too. Tonight she looks like a tree.
The morning will paint her pine needle

comfort on my feet. November snow
burns her face to moon, more ritual
than sage. I drain a deer to stain her lips,

leave the carcass wet on the floor.
I hear talk of green witches. There is
no such thing. Every witch is red.

The Shape of a Hand

My hand starts cramping in the shape of a pen.
The same thing has happened to my mother,
twenty-six years on a crank.
Open the door, close it. Move the shift into place.
Two blocks on, do it again.
Driving buses has made her carpal.
There is a pinch between her back & and her knee.
She is holding out for sixty-five. Every year
a mandatory exam & the doctor threatens to fail her.
Diabetes goes untreated.
High blood pressure, high risk.
What if you have a heart attack while driving?
What about those kids?
She can't afford the medicine,
can barely afford the exam.
Her employer clicks his tongue. Demands
forty-five hours a week paid as forty.
At night I watch her sleep, watch her arm extend
to swing the red stop sign
& allow her children another safe passage.

Featherlungs

I don't want to be a cornflower
girl, all blue in the face. I can't keep
holding my breath around things
that ask for breath held. Today I saw
three cardinals sitting like post-it notes
in the tree outside my apartment. They said
call your grandmother and flew off
in a cross. On the phone she tells me things
she has and hasn't told me. She is angry
for her ladder, the ladder stolen from her yard
or just missing. She asks me what's new
and I say not much. She wants books
for Christmas, nothing else. Has a list
to show me at Thanksgiving. The line
is muzzled by coughing. She says she can't
talk between fits. I say I love you
she coughs. Love you too.

the answer to that question

my intentions lie
on the floor of the truck.
I arrange ladybug parts
along the dashboard,
watch each felted leg pick
angels in the gray.
a white hum replaces
snow. the windshield is cracked
into a spider from when
my sister's boyfriend
mistook it for a drum.
he often mistakes
things for drums. I talk
through her until I stop
talking altogether. she is
eight years older than me.
my nephew is thirteen now.
the next five years are card towers
stacked in neat rows
on the gravel outside. I cannot
reverse nor cut for fear
of them falling, so I allow
the engine to idle. it is warm
enough.

The Bad Orange

There are men & there are men.
The difference is
one beats you & one doesn't.
I hand you two oranges,
ask you to guess
which will slip under your feet
one night & kill you.
The oranges are identical.
The oranges are the same orange.
I spend all morning grinding
peels into zest, pulping out
a juice that can be digested.
The oranges feel attacked
for their orangeness.
Soon all the apples look like oranges,
my hands look like oranges,
there's an orange-shaped bruise
under my sister's right eye.
I write poems denoting the evils
of the orange, the bad orange,
how they can't be trusted.
Go to sleep under shelves of oranges
with an orange curled against my back.

To The Point

If you touch my sister again
I'll blow your head open.

In This Story   pt. 3

In this story I pull his tongue
through the clench of his teeth.
He is awake & I am sleeping.
My sister kneads the tonguemeal
sitting raw on the counter,
pulses it into goose-pimpled dough.
Our kitchen smells of warm
bread, nutmeg, clementine.
There is a surplus of heat. She opens
the low-rested window
to a sky polluted orange. Arachne
crawls the sill seeking refuge.
I take her luck in hand & tuck her
in the cupboard. A snake, a pomegranate,
the spider form a triptych of dust.
In the corner a false mouse in a false
trap. Its back broken & eye bulged.
A reminder: all our goddesses
were fed to us as pea soup.

To-do

You stop writing long enough
to make your fist a hammer.
There is always a demand
demanding, a sink crowded,
socks littering the floor.
The men want more theory,
ask for the material. You don't
want to write for them. They
take this as you can't write.
No one wants to read
a dozen navel-gazing poems
about your mother. No man
wants to read them. You keep
writing your obsession like
the world is anchored in it.
You keep seeing matrilineal
cracks in your ceiling plaster.
It collapses upward to reveal
the entirety of Galileo's attempt
at Dante's universe. One trillion
stars in the shape of your mother,
your best friend's mother,
your sister, grandmother, aunt.
A Botticelli of dust & gas.
The night sky full with pooled
brushstrokes. You try to paint
it permanent but can't imitate
the form. When did you stop
sketching? It's easy to not do
things when there are so many
things to do.

Portrait of an Ill Man

Like the minotaur, he was created
by one betrayal
followed by another.
I've repainted him many times,
each layer as dark as forgiveness.
There's an erosive quality
to acrylic. It can only be built up
so much before it needs time
set aside to dry.
If you paint wet on wet
the underlayers will catch & drag.
Pigment removes pigment.
Here where a painting once sat
lies a colorless body.
When I sleep I drink him down
in specks of corroded pipe
lining my water glass.

The Same Man

The reindeerman was once a little boy
whose dad fed him olives, who laid
out on sunwarm cement & stared
at the clouds til he floated off
into the sky.

He didn't grow antlers until many suns
& stars had snuffed out his eyes.
It may be that his mother taught him
soft lies by absence & his brother,
fists full of cat fur & fire, taught him.

I like to think of the reindeerman as a man
& a boy, lost. The boy got lost in the
man, the same man. & the man spent
too many years trying to find him, casting
yellow beams around his insides until he
lost the trail, too. & then the reindeer

came, took them both up in its antlers
& promised to let them keep bumbling
around in there, from a safe distance.
He guaranteed a shell with warm, thick fat
& a coat worth hanging. Sat them
in his belly & started digesting.

A Christmas Story

The first movie I ever saw was my dad falling off the roof, trailed by string lights. The snow caught him but didn't soften the noise—a heavy blanket with bones inside. The reindeer came next, all wick-thin metal, muzzle blinking warm white. Mom found them like that, an arm in a chest, hoof caging knee, some rejected holiday animorph. She told me to get back inside, but I didn't. I watched her try to pull the two apart. Each tug brought a groan from one of them. Each progress thwarted by a new entanglement. It was like working out the knots in a fine-chained necklace. Lots of patience and a needle required. My mom had neither, so she went for the gardening shears. Had to pick which one to save. The case of my father sat gnarled in the lawn for days.

An Order of Protection

You thought
if I didn't cross the street
I would be okay.
Your generation learned
it could be anybody,
& mine learned.
All there was, to build
the house sturdy.
A lock on every door
surmounted by another.
How do I break your heart?
It was all you had left
to keep us safe.
There was nothing
you could have done.

From Here

I am not trying to run away from anything,
rather into something. Yesterday
it was a parked car, today
the sun. I am running because my mother
taught me to walk. I'm skeptical
of any love that isn't full
of what I don't want to be. In my phone
a list of places to run into: the lake, the border,
a grove full of oranges.
When I bite into an orange
I think this is all I want. The whole world
could be oranges, if it isn't already.

Harley Anastasia Chapman holds an MFA in poetry from Columbia College Chicago & a BA in English with a focus on women & gender studies from Illinois State University. In 2019 she was awarded the Allen & Lynn Turner commencement poetry prize. Her work can be found in *Bridge Eight Press, Euphemism, Soundings East, & Columbia Poetry Review*, among others. Born & raised in rural Illinois, she now resides in Chicago.